T0419160

Learning Map Skills

How to Read a Map

KERRI MAZZARELLA

A Crabtree Roots Plus Book

CRABTREE
Publishing Company
www.crabtreebooks.com

School-to-Home Support for Caregivers and Teachers

This book helps children grow by letting them practice reading. Here are a few guiding questions to help the reader with building his or her comprehension skills. Possible answers appear here in red.

Before Reading:

• What do I think this book is about?
  • *I think this book is about the symbols on a map and what they mean.*
  • *I think this book is about how important it is to know how to read a map.*

• What do I want to learn about this topic?
  • *I want to learn more about how to draw a map.*
  • *I want to learn how to measure distance on a map.*

During Reading:

• I wonder why...
  • *I wonder why scale is included on a map.*
  • *I wonder why there are so many symbols on a map.*

• What have I learned so far?
  • *I have learned that the map key shows symbols and what they mean.*
  • *I have learned that we use the scale to measure distance between two places.*

After Reading:

• What details did I learn about this topic?
  • *I have learned that the title of the map tells what the map is a picture of.*
  • *I have learned that the compass rose shows directions on a map.*

• Read the book again and look for the vocabulary words.
  • *I see the word **tools** on page 3 and the word **locate** on page 8. The other vocabulary words are found on page 23.*

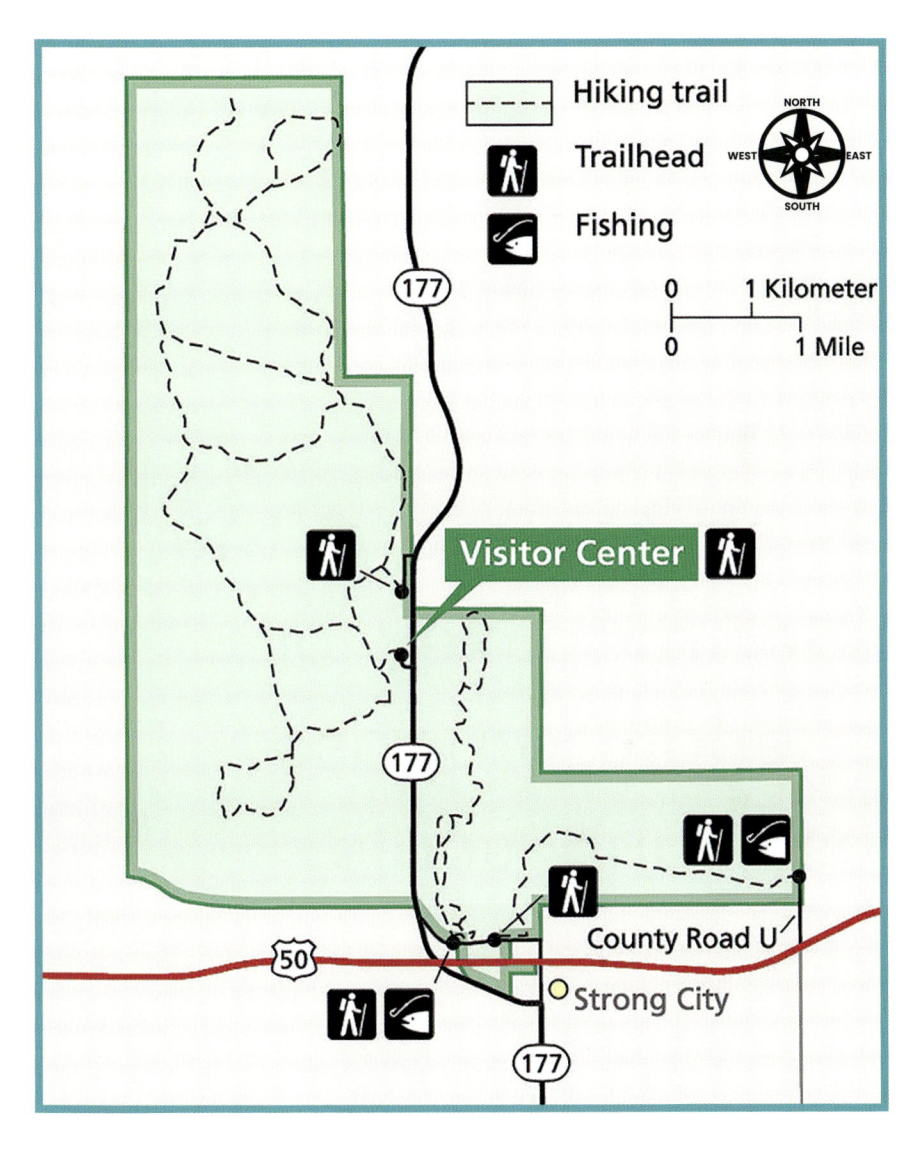

Special **tools** help us read a map.

These tools are the **title**, map key or legend, compass rose, and scale.

title

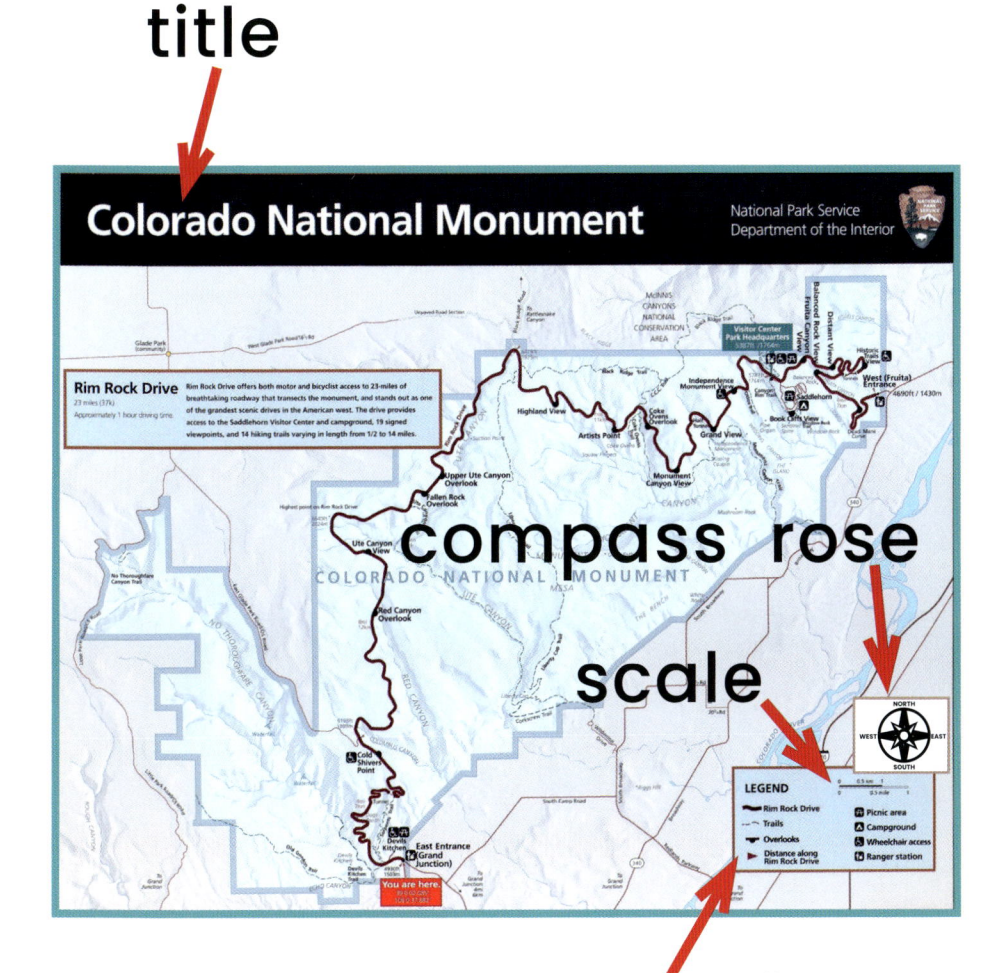

Colorado National Monument

National Park Service
Department of the Interior

Rim Rock Drive

compass rose

scale

map key or legend

MOUNT DESERT ISLAND

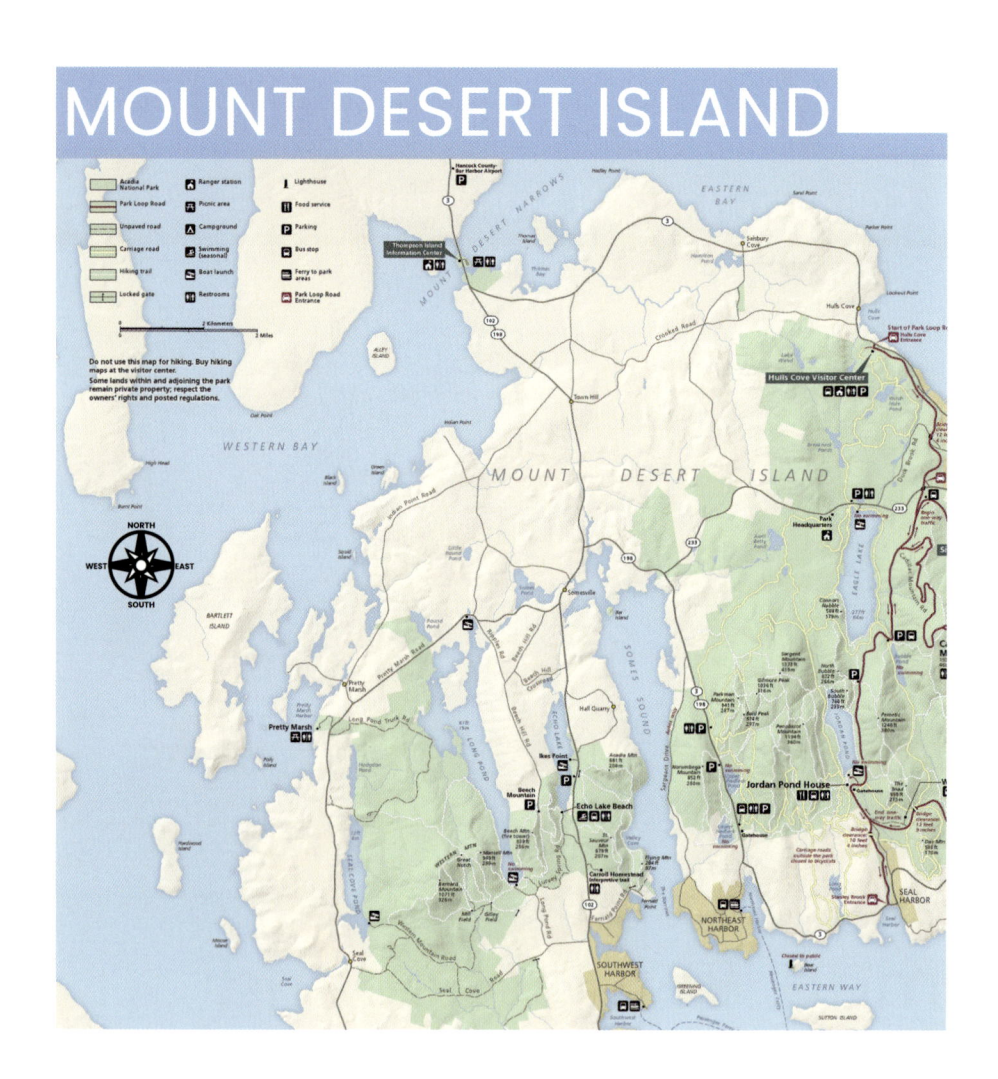

The title says what the map is a picture of.

Can you **locate** the title, map key or legend, compass rose, and scale?

Waterfall Glen
Forest Preserve

A map key or legend shows symbols and says what they mean.

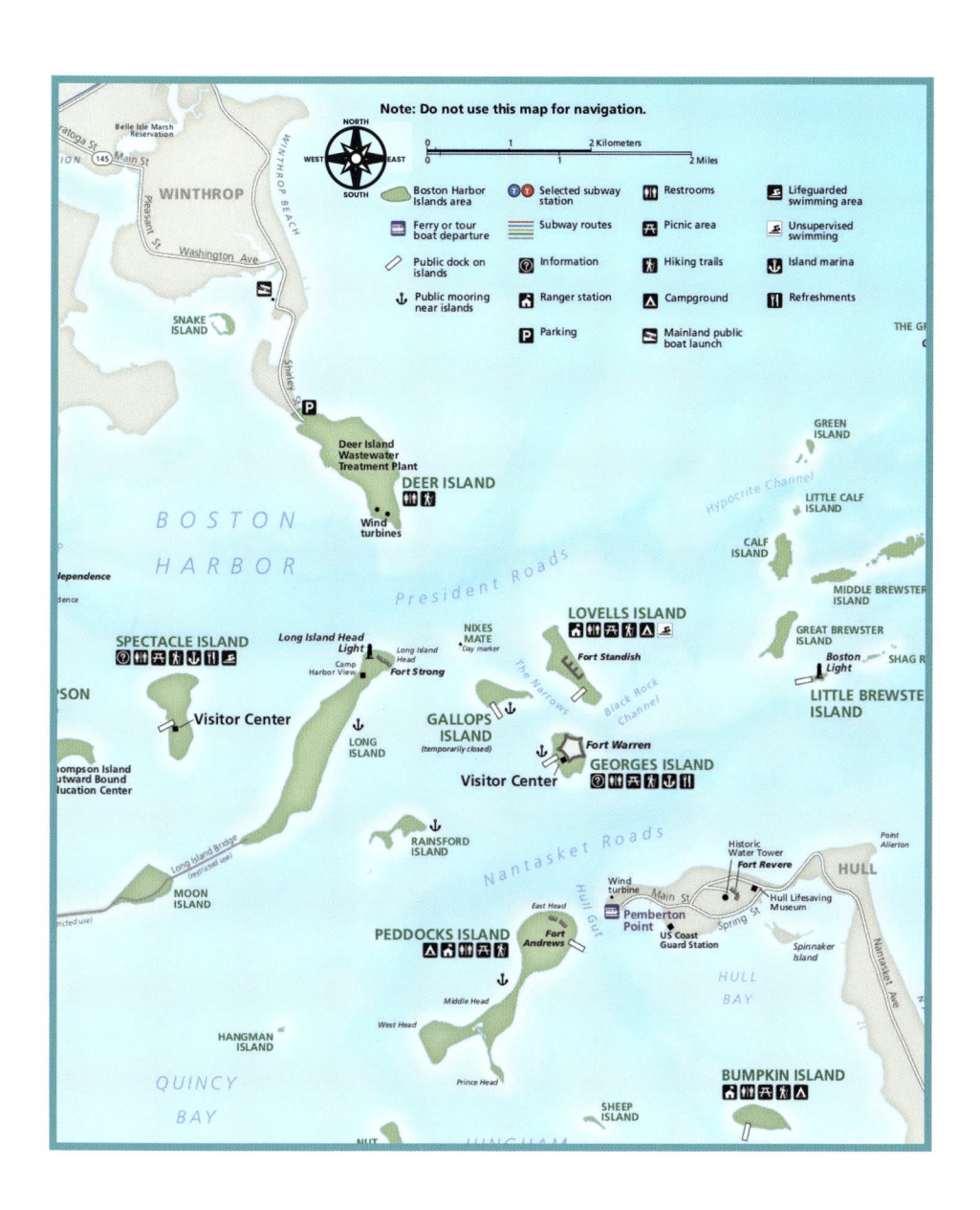

Note: Do not use this map for navigation.

WINTHROP

Belle Isle Marsh Reservation

SNAKE ISLAND

BOSTON HARBOR

Deer Island Wastewater Treatment Plant

DEER ISLAND

Wind turbines

President Roads

Independence

SPECTACLE ISLAND

Visitor Center

THOMPSON

Thompson Island Outward Bound Education Center

Long Island Head Light
Long Island Head
Camp Harbor View
Fort Strong

LONG ISLAND

NIXES MATE
Day marker

The Narrows

LOVELLS ISLAND
Fort Standish

GALLOPS ISLAND
(temporarily closed)

Fort Warren

GEORGES ISLAND

Visitor Center

Black Rock Channel

Long Island Bridge (restricted use)

MOON ISLAND

RAINSFORD ISLAND

Nantasket Roads

PEDDOCKS ISLAND
Fort Andrews

East Head

Middle Head

West Head

HANGMAN ISLAND

QUINCY BAY

Prince Head

SHEEP ISLAND

GREEN ISLAND

Hypocrite Channel

LITTLE CALF ISLAND

CALF ISLAND

MIDDLE BREWSTER ISLAND

GREAT BREWSTER ISLAND

Boston Light

SHAG R

LITTLE BREWSTE ISLAND

THE GR

Historic Water Tower
Fort Revere

Wind turbine
Pemberton Point
US Coast Guard Station

Main St

Point Allerton

HULL

Hull Lifesaving Museum

Spinnaker Island

HULL BAY

BUMPKIN ISLAND

NUT

HINGHAM

Boston Harbor Islands area

Ferry or tour boat departure

Public dock on islands

Public mooring near islands

Selected subway station

Subway routes

Information

Ranger station

Parking

Restrooms

Picnic area

Hiking trails

Campground

Mainland public boat launch

Lifeguarded swimming area

Unsupervised swimming

Island marina

Refreshments

There are symbols for water, trees, and buildings.

GRASS FIELD

SEA

FOREST

POLICE STATION

FIRE STATION

HOSPITAL

LIBRARY

POST OFFICE

The compass rose shows four **directions**: north, south, east, and west.

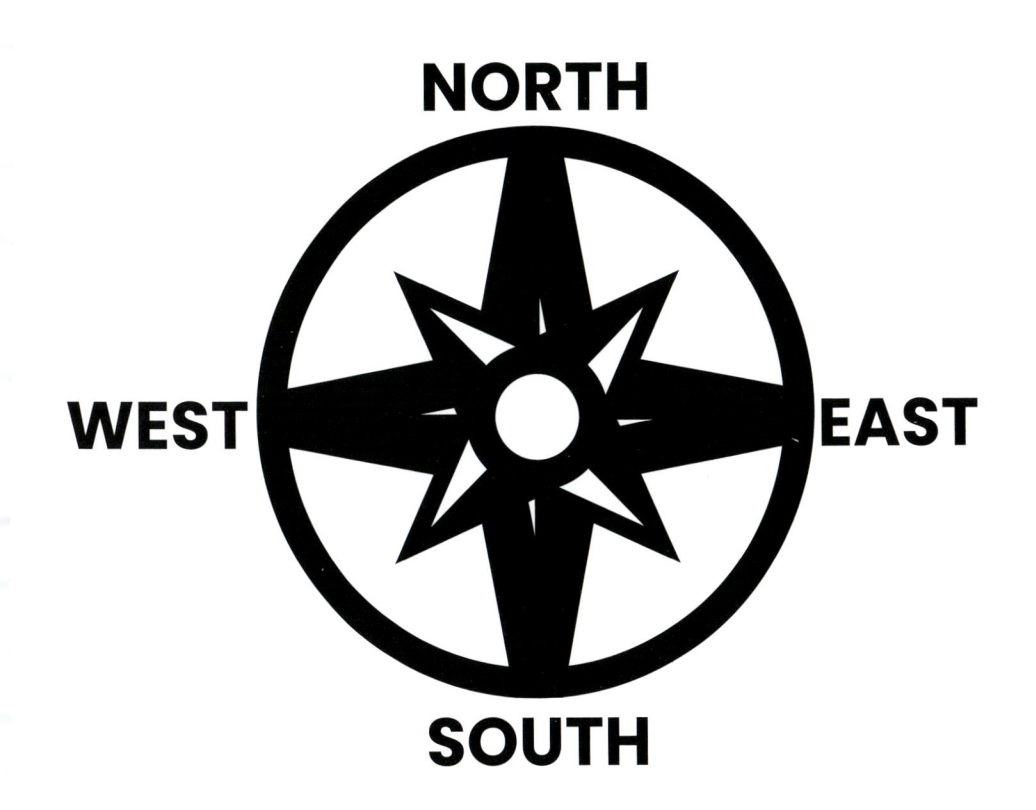

NORTH

WEST

EAST

SOUTH

Use the scale to **measure** the **distance** from one place to another.

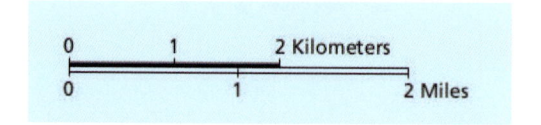

What is located to the north of the lake?

MAP LEGEND

- Forest
- Lake
- Wetland
- Campground
- Stream
- Hiking Trail
- Road

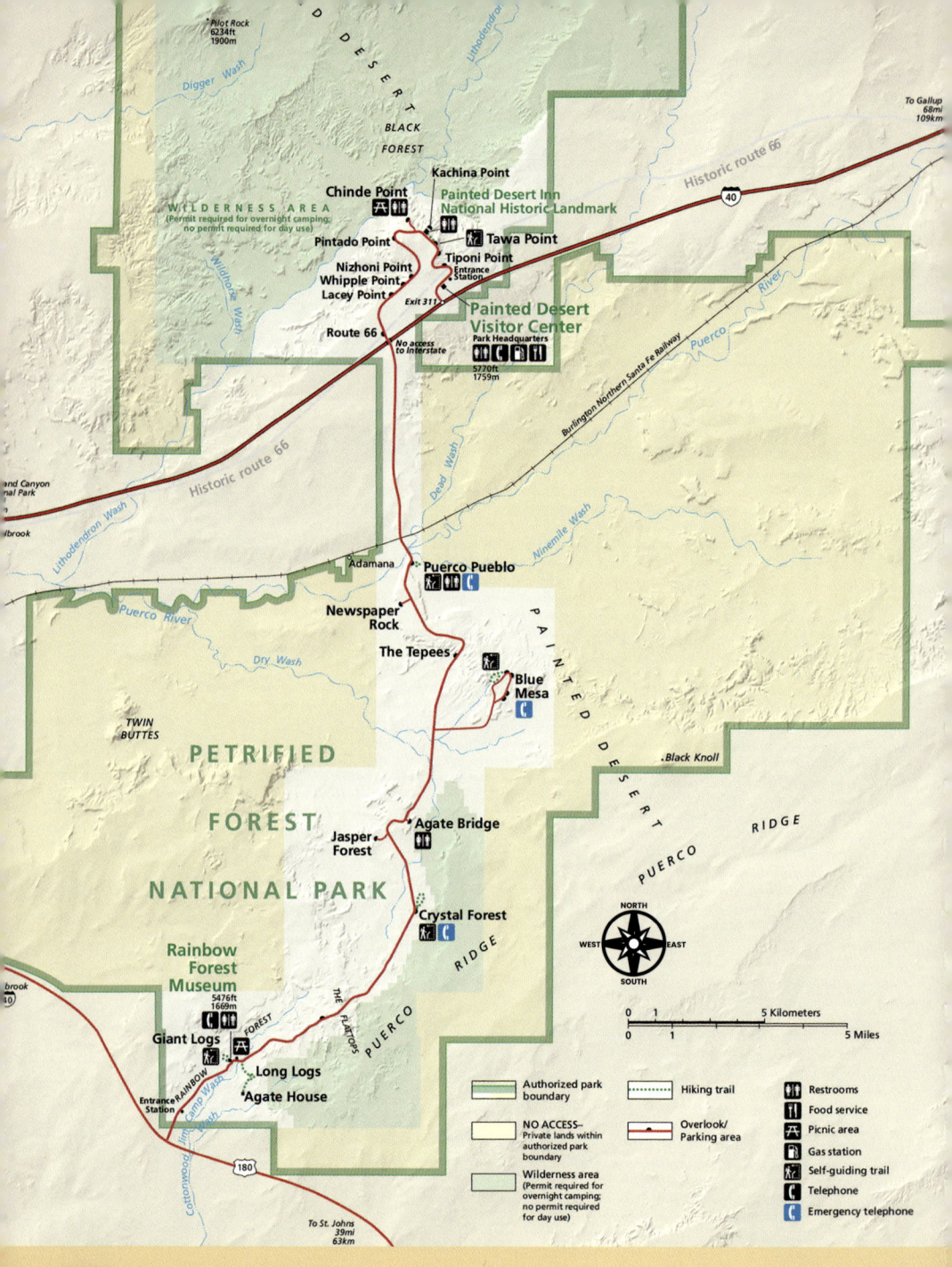

Pilot Rock
6234ft
1900m

PAINTED DESERT

BLACK

FOREST

Digger Wash

Lithodendron Wash

To Gallup
68mi
109km

Historic route 66

40

WILDERNESS AREA
(Permit required for overnight camping;
no permit required for day use)

Chinde Point

Kachina Point
Painted Desert Inn
National Historic Landmark

Pintado Point

Tawa Point

Nizhoni Point
Whipple Point
Lacey Point

Tiponi Point
Entrance
Station

Puerco River

Route 66

Exit 311

No access
to Interstate

Painted Desert
Visitor Center
Park Headquarters
5570ft
1759m

Burlington Northern Santa Fe Railway

Historic route 66

and Canyon
al Park

Lithodendron Wash

Ilbrook

Puerco River

Dead Wash

Ninemile Wash

Adamana

Puerco Pueblo

Newspaper
Rock

Dry Wash

The Tepees

PAINTED DESERT

Blue
Mesa

TWIN
BUTTES

PETRIFIED

FOREST

Black Knoll

NATIONAL PARK

Jasper
Forest

Agate Bridge

PUERCO RIDGE

Crystal Forest

RIDGE

Rainbow
Forest
Museum
5476ft
1669m

THE FLATTOPS

FOREST

Puerco

NORTH
WEST EAST
SOUTH

Giant Logs

RAINBOW

Long Logs

Entrance
Station

Camp Wash

Agate House

0   1   5 Kilometers
0   1   5 Miles

brook
40

Cottonwood

Jim Camp Wash

180

To St. Johns
39mi
63km

	Authorized park boundary			Hiking trail			Restrooms
	NO ACCESS— Private lands within authorized park boundary			Overlook/ Parking area			Food service
	Wilderness area (Permit required for overnight camping; no permit required for day use)						Picnic area
							Gas station
							Self-guiding trail
							Telephone
							Emergency telephone

20

What do you see on
the map?

Word List

Sight Words

a	legend	symbols
and	map	tell
another	mean	the
are	of	there
east	one	these
for	picture	they
from	read	to
help	says	us
is	scale	west
key	shows	you
lake	special	

Words to Know

directions

distance

locate

measure

title

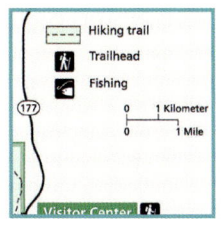

tools

Learning Map Skills

How to Read a Map

Written by: Kerri Mazzarella

Designed by: Rhea Wallace

Series Development: James Earley

Proofreader: Petrice Custance

Educational Consultant: Marie Lemke M.Ed.

Photographs:

Shutterstock: Mister Din: cover, p. 1; NPS: p. 3, 6, 11, 17, 20; EQRay: p. 5; K Ramirez: p. 9; Leremy: p. 13; Natalia Bahmut: p. 15; Dmitry Nikiforov: p. 17e

Library and Archives Canada Cataloguing in Publication

CIP available at Library and Archives Canada

Library of Congress Cataloging-in-Publication Data

CIP available at Library of Congress

Crabtree Publishing Company

Printed in the USA/072022/CG20220201

www.crabtreebooks.com   1-800-387-7650

Published in the United States
Crabtree Publishing
347 Fifth Avenue, Suite 1402-145
New York, NY, 10016

Published in Canada
Crabtree Publishing
616 Welland Ave.
St. Catharines, ON, L2M 5V6